AF375492

# The Fallen Leaf

## Wendy

### Written and Illustrated by J.C. Villalon

To Ashe and the amazing friends in the trans community for their invaluable insights into the complexities of transgender issues. Your openness and wisdom were the guiding lights that propelled me to complete this book. May this work contribute to a world of understanding and celebration of the diverse human experiences.

www.TheFallenLeafBook.com

"A caterpillar. Sometimes I want to be
just like you. I would hide away in my
cocoon and wish that when I came
out, I'd be someone else."

"I would fly away to find the Happy
Place."

"Sometimes I feel defeated and unsure. I don't know who I am and if this is the right path."

"An owl!
Hello. I think I'm lost."

"You are not lost," said the owl.
"Everything you're doing is just as it should be.
Don't give up.
Carry on and the light will lead you."

"There's the light.
Will you stay with me while I sleep?
I'm afraid of the dark."

"Thank you and goodbye."

"It's a new morning.
A new day. And a new life."

"I have long hair now, just like I dreamed of.
Dreams do come true.
I hope the boy can forgive me."

"I feel so sad today," said the girl, as she waved the boy goodbye. "Why was I born this way?"

"Hello. Are you a friend?" the girl
asked someone with a kind smile.

"I am a friend, and I love you just the
way you are."

"Did you see the boy?" asked the girl,
worried. "I hope I didn't make him sad.
I hope I didn't hurt him."

"The boy is fine," said the Friend.
"He said he loves you very much.
He wants you to be  happy."

"An opossum!
You don't need to pretend you're dead.
I promise I won't hurt you."

"Oh, that's a relief," said the opossum. "Thank you!"

"Sometimes I don't understand why I feel so different from everyone else," said the girl.

"We come in various shapes and sizes," said the opossum. "Being different is what makes the world a special place. Catch! A fallen leaf. So colorful and so beautiful."

"It's a dead leaf," said the girl.

"It's not dead," said the opossum. "It's full of life. It falls to the ground and nourishes the soil. It's for you."

"Thank you," said the girl. "I'll keep it close to my heart."

"I've been looking for the light," said the
girl. "It was up there, but now it's gone."

"There's the stag," said the opossum.
"He ought to know."

"Can you help me find the light?" asked
the girl. "I can't see it anymore."

"The light is here," reassured the stag.
"It's warm and bright. It's all around you."

"Why can't I see it?" asked the girl.
"Sometimes you need to look deep
within yourself to find it," said the stag.

"What if it's gone?" asked the girl, worried.
"It can't be," the stag insisted. "It's far too strong to
be extinguished. Don't give up."

"Sometimes all I want to do is give up."

"We'll be by your side to make sure you don't,"
said the opossum.

"I hear someone crying."

"Look, it's a cute little duckling," said the girl.
Why are you crying?"

"I'm lonely and afraid," the duckling answered.
"I so wish to belong somewhere."

"There's a special place where we all belong. It's called Home. If we stick together, we'll find it."

"I feel so shy. Ashamed even," said the girl.
"I feel lost again."

"We all feel that way sometimes. The truth is you are amazing in every way. Find the light and strength inside you," said the stag.

"The light. It's back!"

"I was so afraid I'd never see you again.
These are my friends.
Can you show us the way?"

"Look. Down there," said the duckling. "Warmth."
"Is that the Happy Place?" asked the opossum.
"I believe it is the Happy Place," said the girl.

"Someone's waiting for us," said the stag.

"You made it," greeted the Friend at the doorway.
"We've been expecting you."

"Do you know about me?" asked the girl.
"Yes, we all do. We knew you'd find your way."

"And you'll let me stay? Just as I am?" asked the girl.
"Especially as you are," answered the Friend.
"Are there others here like me?"
"Yes, everyone."

"Then this must be the Happy Place," said the girl.
"Are we family now?"
"We are family," they all agreed.

"Welcome home!"

Support your local library, they shine a bright
light in every community

Celebrate your teachers and librarians, they
can help you shine your brightest.